Pope Urban VIII and Pope Alexander VII: Selected Poetry

Pope Urban VIII and Pope Alexander VII: Selected Poetry

Lyrical Musings of Two Baroque Pontiffs

Freely adapted into English heroic verse by
ROBERT NIXON

RESOURCE *Publications* • Eugene, Oregon

POPE URBAN VIII AND POPE ALEXANDER VII: SELECTED POETRY
Lyrical Musings of Two Baroque Pontiffs

Copyright © 2020 Robert Nixon. All rights reserved. Except for brief quotations in critical publications or reviews, no part of this book may be reproduced in any manner without prior written permission from the publisher. Write: Permissions, Wipf and Stock Publishers, 199 W. 8th Ave., Suite 3, Eugene, OR 97401.

Resource Publications
An Imprint of Wipf and Stock Publishers
199 W. 8th Ave., Suite 3
Eugene, OR 97401

www.wipfandstock.com

PAPERBACK ISBN: 978-1-7252-7303-0
HARDCOVER ISBN: 978-1-7252-7304-7
EBOOK ISBN: 978-1-7252-7305-4

Manufactured in the U.S.A.   06/04/20

Souvent la vision du Poète me frappe:
Ange à cuirasse fauve, il a pour volupté
L'éclair du glaive, ou, blanc songeur, il a la chape,
La mitre byzantine et le bâton sculpté.

—Stéphane Mallarmé, 1862

"In vision oft the Poet I behold,
As angel clad in luminescent gold,
Who joyously delights, in fancied play,
To show the falchion's keen, chalybdic ray;
Or else, in ornamental cope's rich gleam,
With miter byzantine encrowned, to dream;
To wield the rhabdos of a Pontiff's power,
With orphic pen to muse away the hour."

Contents

Translator's Introduction | ix

SELECTED POETRY OF POPE URBAN VIII | 1

   The Flight from Vanity and the Love of Eternity | 3
   After the Death by Execution of Mary, Queen of Scots | 5
   On the Words of St. Augustine: *Inquietum est cor nostrum
      donec requiescat in te . . .* | 6
   To the City of Rome, on the Death of
      Cardinal Alessandro Farnese | 7
   True Wisdom: The Contemplation of Death | 8
   In Praise of the Countryside | 10
   On the Wondrous Variety of Flowers
      Blooming one Winter Time | 12
   The Banderole of Charity | 13
   Inscription for a Bronze Dragon in the Garden
      of Cardinal Scipione Borghese | 15
   The Emptiness of Learning without Piety | 16
   The Agitation of the Depraved Soul, Compared with the
      Quiet Peace of the Righteous | 18
   On the Birthday of Christ our Lord | 20
   Hymn to the Divine Spirit | 21
   The Sun and the Bee | 23
   On the Engagement Ring of the Blessed Virgin Mary,
      Reverently Preserved in the City of Perugia | 24
   On the Work of Cardinal Robert Bellarmine,
      The Ascension of the Mind into God | **25**
   Ode for St. Mary Magdalene | 27
   On a Statue of the Huntress Goddess Diana by a Fountain | 30

SELECTED POETRY OF POPE ALEXANDER VII | 31

    To Poetry | 33
    On the Day of the Annunciation of the Conception of the
       Lord to the Blessed Virgin Mary | 34
    On the Election of Urban VIII as Pope | 35
    Inscription for an Unnamed Tomb I | 36
    Inscription for an Unnamed Tomb II | 37
    On a Copy of Caesar's *Commentaries* which has been
       Gnawed by a Mouse | 38
    On Water Turning into Stone, and Stone into Water | 39
    On Rome | 40
    Meditation on the Nativity of Christ | 41
    Meditation on the Passion of the Savior I: *'Ecce Homo'* | 43
    Meditation on the Passion of the Savior II:
       In the Garden of Gethsemane | **44**
    A Prayer to God Imploring his Assistance | 45
    An Inscription for a Tomb Composed in the
       Style of the Tenth Century | 46
    A Note Accompanying a Cat,
       Given as a Gift to a Young Woman | 47
    A Note Accompanying a Rose
       Given as a Gift to a Young Woman | 49
    A Pilgrimage to a Shrine of the Virgin Mary | 50

Translator's Introduction

Ad Lectorem benevolentem...

THIS VOLUME PRESENTS, FOR the first time, English verse translations of a selection of poetry written by two popes of the baroque era—Urban VIII and Alexander VII. Each of these held the reins of governance of the Roman Catholic Church during the seventeenth century. Urban VIII, born Maffeo Barberini in 1568, occupied the papal throne from 1623 until his death in 1644. Alexander VII (1599–1667), baptized as Fabio Chigi, was elected pope in 1655, and exercised the petrine ministry for the remainder of his mortal life.

    The selection contained herein comprises a choice cornucopia of items which are both rare literary curiosities and ornately fashioned treasures of the most exalted and virtuosic poetical art. The era and cultural milieu from which they sprang—baroque Italy of the seventeenth century—was one in which poetry and literature flourished with all the orichalch splendor of a radiant and sometimes extravagant opulence; and yet which, today, has been rendered caliginously obscure by the dust of accumulated neglect. Indeed, issues of linguistic, literary and cultural alterity—and, to an extent, deliberate prejudice—have each contributed to the casting of an opaque (or at least only marginally translucent) pall over these arcane treasures. It is the intention of this present small work of translation and adaptation boldly to lift this tenebrous veil, diligently to re-polish the aureate, marble or onyx surfaces of the artworks concealed thereby, and humbly to offer their gilded arabesques and argent-spangled trefoils to the discerning eye of a modern, Anglophone reading public.

    Both Urban VIII and Alexander VII were from the same social and cultural circles—circles distinguished by affluence, nobility, influence, culture, talent and learning. Additionally, both were close personal friends, united by a bond of common literary interests and shared poetical aspirations.

The world in which they lived was, of course, very different from our own. Nepotism, privilege, extravagance and luxury were taken for granted amongst such elites. But it is perhaps prudent not to be excessively hasty in casting retrospective moral judgements. This was, after all, simply the environment and culture to which they had been born. Certainly, neither of these pontiffs were a saint, a mystic, or a zealot; but each was, in his own way, devoutly faithful, highly imaginative, profoundly learned and vividly sensitive to truth and beauty.

In the world immediately succeeding the Renaissance and still basking in the refulgence of its glories, literary education—specifically the study of the Latin and Greek classics—enjoyed firm primacy of place amongst the human accomplishments, especially in Italy. To many modern readers, the idea that a thorough immersion in the *Aeneid* and Anacreon, Pindar and Pliny, Horace and Homer, Caesar and Cicero (and all the intricacies of grammar, rhetorical devices and poetic metrics concomitant thereto), constituted the best possible formation for ecclesiastic or civil office—and, for that matter, cultivated life in general—may well seem to be a little far-fetched. But such was the prevalent view in Italy in the sixteenth and seventeenth centuries, and apparently neither unfruitful nor ineffective in the remarkable social, cultural and political results it produced. Perhaps, indeed, there is some wisdom in Plato's maxim; "The true object of education is to teach us to love the beautiful."

Both Urban VIII and Alexander VII confess in their own writings that poetry was for them their constant source of solace, and also the field of endeavor in which they took their greatest personal pride. Alexander, for example, expresses his attraction to the poetic art thus:

> *I'll follow not the stirring call of arms,*
> *Nor clarion blasts, resounding fierce alarms,*
> *Nor promises of treasuries untold*
> *Awaiting for the navigator bold.*
> *But rather lulling tones of rippling rills*
> *My heart with gentler yearnings now do fill.*
> *Nor martial praise, nor bloodied victories,*
> *This poet's soul could evermore appease. (. . .)*

> *For what is life indeed but one great song,*
> *A stream which wanders ceaselessly along?*
> *A glass of Lethe's wine, an ode of Horace,*
> *Serve me as anodyne, suffice for solace.*

Translator's Introduction   xi

Urban, writing to a certain youthful nephew, gently but sagaciously reprimands him for applying himself with an excessive ardor to the acquirement of literary accomplishments, and falling prey to an overly ambitious drive to achieve fame as a poet. Yet he quite candidly admits himself guilty of precisely the same tendencies, and similar poetic aspirations.

> *And thus, methinks, it may well be for thee—*
> *Who labor like a modern Hercules*
> *To master Latin and the Attic tongue,*
> *Stupendous feats for one yet still so young;*
> *And do so that thou thereby may acquire*
> *Rich elegance of speech and lyric fire,*
> *Which shall equip thee well to take thy seat*
> *Amongst the poets, whom the Muses greet.*
>
> *Yet wherefore is it—often do I muse—*
> *That human minds so ardently enthuse*
> *To take their rest in heliconian glades,*
> *To glory in the laurel's pensive shades?*
>
> *We seek—I too!—a palm whose fruit is sorrow,*
> *As if from deathless verse we life could borrow,*
> *As if undying words could breath bestow*
> *To mortal remnants clothed in dust below.*

But if such literary ambition is a form of vanity, it is, at least, a relatively innocuous one, as far as vanities go. Moreover, it is by no means wholly incongruous with more profound spiritual aspirations:

> *To sing in golden voice, to sound the lyre*
> *With all that high Parnassus may inspire*
> *Are works, indeed, of sweet felicity,*
> *But lead to naught of true eternity. (. . .)*
>
> *But they who learning and good deeds unite,*
> *With twofold wings shall blithely take their flight;*
> *Their names the Muses will inscribe in stone;*
> *Their souls in Light divine shall find a home!*

The *weltanschauung* which underlies the spirituality of both of these popes, despite its often elaborate and labyrinthine expressions, was—like that of most Catholics of the Renaissance and baroque periods—fundamentally marvelously simple: that the things of this material world are all ephemeral and illusory, and lead to no meaningful satisfaction; whereas it is the things of eternity—the unseen and incomprehensible glory of the transcendent—which are the human heart's true desire and the only real source of substantial and enduring felicity. Thus opines the world-weary Barberini, with a somber but appealing touch of Byronic melancholy and Baudelairean lassitude:

> *Nor gold, nor fame, nor any earthly thing*
> *Our hearts to satisfaction ever bring.*
> *Nor dignity, nor mortal glory's meed*
> *The restless soul to true contentment lead. (. . .)*
> *Know thou that peace is here not to be found,*
> *That lasting bliss bides not on earthly ground.*
>
> *But rather turn thine eyes to things above,*
> *To realms of holy bliss and sacred love,*
> *For there alone can peace enduring be,*
> *In God's supreme, divine eternity.*

In the context of this supramundane orientation, a focus on the aesthetic side of life—be it poetry, art, liturgy, architecture or even physical human beauty—made perfect sense, since perceptible beauty—whether natural or artistic—offered a glimpse (*per speculum in aenigmate*) of the imperceptible, eternal beauty of the Divinity. The aestheticism of the outlook of these two pontiffs might be described as the diametrical (yet mysteriously and paradoxically complementary) antithesis of Puritanism, then prevailing so strongly in many other parts of Europe. Both were (and are) expressions of a longing for something utterly transcending the commonplace and quotidian realities of mere earthly existence.

Viewed through modern eyes, it is perhaps somewhat tempting to interpret the abundant employment of images drawn from classical mythology as symptomatic of a kind of tendency to syncretism, or the ascendency of a veiled (or even overt) neo-Paganism. But such a suggestion would have seemed utterly absurd to a person of the Renaissance, at least in Italy. It was precisely because classical allusions were part of a common and conventional literary and artistic currency that a poet who described the sun as "Apollo's fiery chariot," or spoke of Heaven as "the elysian meadows" incurred no serious risk whatsoever (at least in Catholic lands) of being accused of neo-Paganism, or of infidelity towards the dogmas of Christianity.

Translator's Introduction xiii

On the contrary, classical literature and mythology were seen as being replete with vatic utterances, mysterious oracles and occult figures anticipating the Christian revelation. After all, did not the hierophantically prescient Virgil himself write of the restoration of a fallen world through a boy-child born of a Virgin?

> *Iam redit et Virgo, redeunt Saturnia regna;*
> *iam nova progenies caelo demittitur alto.*
> *Modo nascenti puero, quo ferrea primum*
> *desinet ac toto surget gens aurea mundo. (. . .)*
> *Ille deum vitam accipiet, divisque videbit*
> *permixtos heroas, et ipse videbitur illis*
> *pacatumque reget patriis virtutibus orbem.*

And could it not very plausibly be the redemptive and expiatory sacrifice of Christ (the "true Sun of justice" and hence the genuine Apollo) to which Horace refers—albeit unknowingly—when, with fatiloquent pen, he wrote thus?

> *Cui dabit partes scelus expiandi*
> *Iuppiter? Tandem venias precamur,*
> *Nube candentes humeros amictus,*
>   *Augur Apollo.*

Despite the prevalent focus on profound spiritual and philosophical matters in the writings of these two baroque pontiffs, there are also abundant and refreshing instances of playful humor and light-hearted wit in evidence. This is apparent, for example, in Urban's ludically epigrammatic poem composed as an inscription for a bronze dragon in the garden of his friend, Cardinal Scipione Borghese. The dragon jestingly protests:

> *For though I bear a fiery dragon's form,*
> *In conduct, I do not adopt its norm. (. . .)*
> *I am no monstrous brimstone-breathing beast,*
> *I seek not to distress, not in the least.*
> *For though my gruesome visage may not show it,*
> *At heart—read thou these lines—I am a poet!*

An even more pronounced degree of levity is displayed in certain poems by Alexander (before he assumed the papal dignity, of course), such as in his verses meditating, in jocular fashion, upon a copy of Caesar's *Commentaries* which had been gnawed by a mouse; or his egregiously humorous note written to accompany a cat given to a young woman as a gift.

In Alexander's verses, more so than those of Urban, one also witnesses the intimate expression of tender sentiments—presumably from works dating from the days of youthful ardor and freedom, prior to his entrance into the clerical state. A wonderful example of this is his brief poetic note attached to a rose presented to another young woman, as an ephebic token of passionate affection and amorous admiration:

> *Accept, O Maid, this rose of scarlet red,*
> *Which has upon my tears and sighs been fed;*
> *My tears and sighs which for thee long did flow*
> *This noble blossom—yea—have caused to grow.*

In Alexander's work one also encounters moments in which the intensity of his religious devotion seems palpably to burn through the formal structure and restrained idiom of metrical verse. This is especially true of his two *Meditations on the Passion of the Savior*, and also in one of his most brief and simple compositions, the *Prayer to God Imploring his Assistance*. In this, the language of learning is entirely put aside, and the deepest yearning of his soul revealed with unaffected humility and piety:

> *Within the secret chamber of mine heart,*
> *I hear the gospel word its Truth impart:*
> *"The one who shall my footsteps humbly tread*
> *Will not be conquered by the darkness dread."*
> *O Lord, walk thou as kindly friend to me,*
> *And to my steps a trusted light e'er be.*
> *Without thee, lo, I stumble and I fall;*
> *Thy strength, thy love, thy wisdom be mine all!*

It is pertinent to provide some information about the source texts, and the translational approach herein adopted. The adaptations presented here take as their sources the Latin texts of the 1726 Oxford edition of the collected poetry of Maffeo Barberini, and the 1666 Paris edition of the *Philomathi* of Fabio Chigi. These editions are both textually reliable and of exemplary legibility. They are, moreover, most fittingly and strikingly beautiful volumes, and splendidly ornate examples of the publisher's and typographer's art. There is evidence that Barberini—perhaps in a manifestation of the poetic vanity to which he confessed—took great personal care over the publication of editions of his verse (including in vernacular Italian translations) during his lifetime, even after he had been elected as pope.

Latin poetry, in its classical and neo-classical forms, typically employs metrical schemes which exceed by far the complexity of those figuring in

Translator's Introduction   xv

traditional English verse. Authors of neo-classical Latin poetry wrote according to precisely determined patterns of syllabic quantity, which few English authors have ever dared approach or emulate (with very rare exceptions—amongst whom Sir Philip Sidney and Algernon Charles Swinburne spring most immediately to mind). The essential feature of neo-classical Latin poetry was thus its elaborate and studied formalism—its careful adherence to precisely determined, and often highly complex, metrical schemes; as well as its opulent vocabulary and scintillatingly evocative repertoire of mythological and literary imagery.

In order best to replicate the effect of this in English, the translator has chosen consistently and unvaryingly to adopt the metrical scheme sometimes referred to as English heroic verse, or—to put it more technically—rhymed couplets of iambic pentameter. This metrical structure is arguably the most conspicuously and unabashedly "formal" of all approaches to English versification, and attained its epitome in the works of Waller, Dryden, Blackmore, Pope, Gray, Parnell, Collins, Savage, and innumerable other seventeenth-century and (especially) eighteenth-century English poets—whose voluminous lyrical outpourings in this metrical medium now repose, largely unread, in dusty tomes in silent and empty libraries. Yet the intrinsic appeal and effectiveness of rhymed couplets of iambic pentameter, both to the ear and to the imagination—with its qualities of balance, regularity and symmetry—continue undiminished to the present time, supported by its easy congruence with the natural rhythms of spoken English. Few will deny that the decasyllabic line possesses an indubitable depth of substance, combined with an agility and flexibility, which renders it a most gratefully malleable and receptive prosodic medium for almost all thoughts and sentiments.

It is earnestly hoped that—at least for some readers—a certain pleasure, consolation, edification—and even, perhaps, a few moments of more profound inspiration—may be derived from this overtly classical and mildly archaic style of verse, with its undulating rise and fall of alternating arsis and thesis, and resignedly but reassuringly regular rhymes. For, as the accomplished Mary Robinson, the leading poetess of the English Della Cruscan movement, so eloquently expresses it:

> *For thou, blest Poesy! With godlike powers*
> *To calm our human miseries, wert given;*
> *When passion rends and hopeless love devours,*
> *By mem'ry goaded, and by frenzy driven,*
> *'Tis thine to guide us 'midst Elysian bowers,*
> *And show the fainting soul a glimpse of Heaven!*

This was most assuredly true for the popes Urban VIII and Alexander VII, to each of whom poetry was a hidden garden of refuge, delight and inspiration, a constant and beloved friend, and the promise and pledge of a supernal and everlasting beauty—hinted at, but never fully seen or realized in this passing and circumscribed earthly life. That the noble thoughts and gentle lyrical musings of these two baroque pontiffs may once more rejoice in the golden radiance of day, and that their verses may again know the vivifying light of reading eyes, is something which is, indeed, most devoutly to be wished. For what they sought and expressed with such polish, elegance and intensity continues deeply to resonate in the human heart. Or at least thus it seems to me,

The humble translator,

Robert Nixon, osb
Abbey of the Most Holy Trinity,
New Norcia, Western Australia

Selected Poetry of Pope Urban VIII

And I with pinions emulous of thine,
Eagle of Jove, that circle the Divine,
Would rise to wider vision, face to face,
With Deity in empyrean space;
Lift to the stars my prayer for Beauty's light,
Standing in pride on Song's transcendent height.

—JOHN MYERS O'HARA (1913)

Barberini displayed a noble magnitude of soul—which was imbued
with both the utmost restraint and most joyous exhilaration—in
both his virtues and his vices. He so loved the Muses that they never
deserted him, nor he them. Even when he was most occupied with the
business of his elevated rank and office, as a second Apollo he received
the Muses' gentle visitations, and lovingly transmitted in verse the
golden secrets they conveyed to him.

—JOHN BARCLAY (1582–1621)

The Flight from Vanity and the Love of Eternity

The gentle warmth of long-awaited spring,
To skies, refreshing newness now does bring.
The vernal breezes summon radiant flowers,
As nubile earth embraces roscid showers.
Now nascent Eos sends forth vibrant light,
And murksome winter's gloaming puts to flight.
Albescent lilies of the blooming field
Their fragrant attars to the calm air yield.
The pinioned choir of welkin-vagrant birds
Pour forth their songs, surpassing mortal words,
And gold-inwrought cadenzas improvise
Whilst soaring unrestrained in sapphire skies.
The crystal brooks their luscious banks now kiss,
While fish of fulgent silver play in bliss
Within the water's sparkling clarity;
Of cares tellurian, supremely free.

But—lo!—soon summer's heat shall fiercely burn
With ardent, acrid fire; and so shall turn
The viridescent meads to shades of gray,
Sweet Flora's rainbow glints to fade away.
The rills, of vitreous transparency,
By squall caloric, soon bereft shall be;
The piscine minions of the bourns will go
To seek the cool, in miry depths below.
The feathered sprites their music then must cease,
And silence shall prevail, but nary peace.
The soil beneath gilt Helios will lie,
Exhausted, parched, fatigued—nigh fain to die.

But seasons ever change, and brumal cold
Will soon arrive, in frigid grasp to hold
The boreal steppe. Its frozen, bloodless reign
Ascendancy unrivalled thence shall gain.
As sleet envelops, in its pallid veil,
The mountain peaks, the vicious, pounding hail
Destruction ruthless wreaks; and falls of snow
The grim, chionic mien of Nature show!
The rivers languish, made anaemic by
The frost-gods regnant in the vapid sky.
Dread Charon shall guidon of pitch upraise,
Night's onyx shade to cast across the days.

Thus fleetly all subastral things are passed;
For nothing here eternally may last.
Its glamors and its boasts are thus all lies,
For that is not true life which quickly dies.
Look rather to the things which do endure;
The vision deiform, which to the pure
Of heart God's mercy shall, at last, bestow,
In bliss which neither end nor close will know.
For there the summer's heat and winter's cold
Shall not afflict, nor change imperium hold,
Eternal light and love's unending day
Possessing perfect, uncontested sway.

All transient toys—O!—learn thou to despise;
And Heaven's sempiternal joys to prize!

After the Death by Execution of Mary, Queen of Scots

O Queen of Scotland brave, and noble daughter
Of holy church, made subject to cruel slaughter!
Thy blood the jealous axe's thirst did slake;
Thou regal state, for Christ's love, didst forsake.
Let not the corvine wing of morbid gloom
Enshroud thy lifeless body, nor thy tomb;
Let rather terror's acheronian night
Upon thy slayers' hearts and lands alight!

For thee, now burns no due somatic flame,
Yet in the gold of stars is writ thy name!
The seraph host resound thy praise on high;
While grief from me commands a silent sigh.

On the Words of St. Augustine:
Inquietum est cor nostrum donec requiescat in te...

Nor gold, nor fame, nor any earthly thing
Our hearts to satisfaction ever bring.
Nor dignity, nor human glory's meed
The restless soul to true contentment lead.
And shall the heart esurient then wage
A search for that which longing may assuage?
In changing things, unchanging peace to know—
The joys which dwell above, in things below?

O soul! Look to thy left and to thy right;
Examine, as thou wilt, both day and night.
Behold, from every side do cares assail;
Peace—constantly chimerical—must fail.
For foe with foe doth bitterly contend;
And never shall such mortal strivings end.
Yea, hope but alternates with dark despair,
And rest is ever sullied by fresh care.
Thus hope—Pandora's teasing, parting gift—
Capriciously the heart may stoop to lift
From depths abyssic, then oft disappears,
Engulfed in galling tides of anxious fears.

All that our worldly blandishments do seem
To offer to the soul, are, as a dream,
But passing phantoms in the depths of night,
Illuminated by mendacious light.
By hebetude deceived, we seek by pains
And labor, from our labor to obtain
Some rest, but ever we do merely find
That labor but begets itself in kind.

Know thou that peace is not here to be found,
That lasting joy bides not on earthly ground.
But rather turn thine eyes to things above,
To realms of holy bliss and sacred love,
For there alone can peace enduring be,
In God's supreme, divine eternity.

To the City of Rome, on the Death of Cardinal Alessandro Farnese

O Rome, eternal Rome, why dost thou weep—
So plaintively threnodial vigil keep?
Beloved Alessandro's purpled splendor,
Their fleshly chains of late—yea—did surrender:
For him, thou raise a stertorous lament,
Whose soul from hence to Heaven has been sent.
For him, thou sound the strains of shawm-toned dirge—
Whose essence, liberated, now does surge
Unto th'elysian meadows, star bedight,
Unto the halls of transcendental light.

Yea, whilst Farnese lived, he did bestow
Upon the church and arts pellucid glow.
Yes, gave he ever with a liberal hand
The means whereby marmoreal chancels stand,
And fanes of jade and jasper did he raise
As long as did perdure his mortal days.
Thus doing, well he merited reward—
An empyrean crown, *in astris* stored.

O Rome, to whom he gave his very best,
Begrudge him not his well-deservéd rest!
Let not his boons, his patronage of art,
More than himself, be cherished in thy heart!
Thy tears withhold; his merits, though, recall,
Who slumbers now in far Olympia's hall!

True Wisdom: The Contemplation of Death

The ever-turning, ever-changing sphere
Of earth draws, each day, to its end more near,
As spinning through the vault of vacant skies
It hastens to its ultimate demise.
Each day and every year's a gravid mother
That soon will render due birth to another;
And as we turn with trembling hand the page
Of daily life's unfolding story, Age—
That gray, unbeauteous harbinger of sorrow—
Is nigher every morn and every morrow.
And youth's strong vigor that abounds today
Doth promise naught, except to pass away.
The somber, tear-drenched, melancholic pall
Of death is cast, insatiate, over all.
Thus silent beasts, which hungrily do graze,
The meadow's verdure ruthlessly erase;
And so the flames, impatient to consume,
In fiery greed the fertile field subsume.

Thus taught the sages from the days of old
The prudent heart, affections to withhold
From passing things, enduring but a day,
And slipping, with fugacious time, away.
Know thou that mortal praise and mortal glory
Is but a fable told, a puerile story:
And that the sateless lust for hylic gold
Is but a snare which jealously would hold
Thy Heaven-destined heart in aureate bond,
Whose true desire remains the realms beyond.

Ye fools and knaves! O, wherefore must you cast
Rapacious gaze on things that cannot last?
Our souls seek not for idle toys terrestrial,
But rather crave ambrosia celestial.
Unto itself the azure Heaven calls us!
How long shall dust and shades serve to enthrall us?

But contemplation of life's empty show
Shall discipline salubrious bestow,
An admonition that all things must pass:
A fragile ptyx is life, akin to glass,
Which breaks and shatters, not to be reformed
By art nor skill, and thus are mortals born
To live and die but once; then be no more,
Consigned to Sheol's depths for evermore.

We are but pilgrims in this fleeting world,
Our lives slip by, like gale-tossed flags unfurled.
So wise the one who's mindfully aware
Of life's brief finitude, and gives his care
To look upon death bravely in the face,
Whilst knowing that in Heaven there's a place
Where his immortal heart may ever rest,
Amongst the multitude of souls made blest,
And there all mortal turbulence shall cease
Dissolved in endless oceans of God's peace.

In Praise of the Countryside

The peaceful fields so gently do invite
Our souls from crowded cities to take flight,
With verdant vistas and with pleasant breeze;
Away from urban strife, to take our ease.
O, wherefore should we in the crowds delay,
And waste, amidst the throng, another day?

Behold! The spring approaches amiably;
Begraced by choriambic melody.
Blue-pinioned swallows soar on graceful wing;
Their odes dulcisonant, delight to sing.
The winter's glacial snowfalls now have vanished,
Its baneful winds and hoarfrosts, too, are banished.
And, lo, the umbrous clouds of darksome hue
Succumb to lepid springtide's crystal dew.
The streams and rills, with turbid rains once gray,
Now hyalescent, glow; ev'n as the day,
With warmly fulgid, chrysoberyl light,
Dispels the dwalming shadows of the night.
Each springtide pleasure temptingly does breathe:
"O, from the dismal city take thy leave!"

The meadows scintillate, smaragdine green.
Both rose and rarest orchid now do seem
Like polished, opalescent precious stones,
In panoply of variegated tones.
The grapevine weaves it gracile branches' web
And, Phoenix-like, now from its mossy bed
Arises to embrace the lambent sun,
While limpid brooks their placid courses run,
And avian choirs, in philomelic lays,
Proclaim, with joy, Persephone's glad praise.
Thus rural fields entreatingly invite
Our souls in green seclusion to respite.

O! Let the pureness of such atmosphere
Be drawn into my panting lungs, and clear
The dross and dregs of urban dust away,
While rident zephyrs all around me play!
The glebes of corn already undulate,
Caressed by playful winds, which permeate
The air with coolness, while refulgent light,
In apricot auroras, dances bright.
Each vernal vision vehemently does urge:
"Thy soul from civic dust strive thou to purge!"

Yea, such resounding peace the mind inspires
To nurture, deep within, the Muse's fires,
Which in the city's moil of busyness,
By stress and mundane care are oft suppressed.
O, wherefore should we in the crowds delay,
And waste, amidst this throng, another day?

It is in rural meadows that we'll find
Nepenthe's balm to lull the burthened mind.
Thus verdant fields do lovingly invite
Thy heart in calm seclusion to respite:
Where temp'rate spring's Edenic gifts abound,
There peace and happy innocence are found!

On the Wondrous Variety of Flowers Blooming one Winter Time

The frosty winds this wintertide rejoice
And sing unwonted lays with silvern voice,
And proudly boast their colorful display
Of floral blooms, which importunely play
Amidst hibernal zephyrs of the air,
Without—it seems—for season's order, care.

But jealous Spring complains resentfully:
"O Lady Winter, thou hast stole from me
This multitude of Flora's pretty glow,
Who in my time, not thine, more aptly show!"

Then Lady Winter does to Spring reply,
"My brother, thy complaint is not a lie.
But please consider this—that thou well know
That thou, too, steal from me my white-hued snow;
My servants, too, the chilly winds and gales,
Within thy season's bounds thou let prevail!"

This colloquy Sir Wisdom interrupts;
"My friends, of this dispute we've heard enough!
O Seasons! Ye are sisters and are brothers,
So meetly share your traits with one another."

The Banderole of Charity

To his brother, Niccolo Barberini

Militia est vita hominis super terram.
—Job 7:1

>Let that which Wisdom often deigns declare
>Be writ upon thy heart with prudent care:
>That for all mortal beings corporeal life
>Is fraught with labor, toil and endless strife.
>For while the soul is bound in sarkic chains,
>It shall be subject to its lot of pains.
>
>Know that the human heart, all of the while
>That here it bides, shall not evade its trial.
>At night, it troubled restlessness shall know;
>Awake, it hunger's gnawings undergo.
>Deceptions shall it find on every side,
>As snares, concealed in hiding, do abide.
>And lust and sin shall seek the soul to harm,
>With beautiful temptations as its arms.
>And wrath shall burn in dark, voracious pyres;
>Ambition, too, shall kindle vain desires.
>With such a multitude of hostile foes,
>Each soul along its path of life must go;
>These boldly all seek ingress to the hall
>Of innocence, to orchestrate its fall.
>
>But fear not, Brother; rather take due care
>With apt defense thy strongholds to prepare,
>To gird thyself with walls of chastity,
>To still thy mind with pure sobriety,
>To tame thy heart with tender piety,
>And vest thy soul with holy charity.
>If with such holy instruments thou shield
>Thyself, then soon thy soul's fierce foes shall yield.

But, Brother mine, do not be self-deceived;
Beware, lest lies of pride should be believed,
For never was more perilous a foe
Then self against the self, that does not know
The carnal motives, lurking deep within,
Which never cease to urge frail flesh to sin.

O Charity! Unconquered force of Love,
Thou fire celestial sent from realms above—
O, free me from temptation's lurid strife
And lead me through the battlefield of life!
I'm safe with thee as mentor and as guide,
Protected with thy wisdom at my side.

O Brother, let not earthly care detain
Thy mind, nor let desires thy heart enchain.
But rather contemplate life's final end,
And let thy thoughts to things eternal tend.
Not they who combat merely once or twice
Or thrice—or many times!—with sin and vice,
As victors, gain their entrance to the high
Sidereal meadows far beyond the sky;
For but one sinful fall is all it takes
To lose felicity's eternal stakes.

Who enters, void of grace, the silent tomb
Shall meet not rest but rather endless doom.
But, with a faithful soul and constant mind,
The path to Light divine thy soul will find—
If both in life and death thou shalt embrace
Supernal Charity's redeeming grace.

Inscription for a Bronze Dragon in the Garden of Cardinal Scipione Borghese

    Despite my fearsome aspect, wrought in gleaming
    And polished bronze, think not, prithee, me seeming
    To frighten thee away, O welcome guest,
    From this abode of pleasant, tranquil rest.
    For though I bear a fiery dragon's form,
    In conduct, I do not adopt its norm.
    No cacodaemon I, of sanguine rite,
    Nor heinous imp of antinomian night;
    Nor incubus of fey Hecate's lore,
    Nor maze-trapped, therionic Minitour;
    Nor Hydra, polycephalous and horrid,
    Nor chthonic wormling, spawned of humors torrid.
    I am no monstrous brimstone-breathing beast;
    I seek not to distress, not in the least.
    For though my gruesome visage may not show it,
    At heart—read thou these lines—I am a poet!

The Emptiness of Learning without Piety

To his young cousin, Giovanni Donato

> The one who from his tender childhood days
> Applies himself to mastery of the waves,
> And who the sailor's hardy craft would learn,
> That on the seas his livelihood may earn,
> Shall soon perceive that transient, human life
> Is like a sea, with tempest and with strife
> Replete, and that the state to which we're born
> Resembles waters churned by vicious storms.
> Long voyages he'll face and ceaseless gales,
> As at the ocean's whim he bravely sails.
> Sharp hunger will he know and bitter thirst,
> And warfare's bloody darts and sword accurst.
>
> Not these shall he who joins the fleet escape,
> But subject be to adamantine Fate.
> For they who peril's hardships would disdain
> Shall never glory's diadem attain.
> And thus, methinks, it may well be for thee—
> Who labor like a modern Hercules
> To master Latin and the Attic tongue,
> Stupendous feats for one yet still so young;
> And do so that thou thereby may acquire
> Rich elegance of speech and lyric fire,
> Which shall equip thee well to take thy seat
> Amongst the poets, whom the Muses greet.
>
> Yet wherefore is it—often do I muse—
> That human minds so ardently enthuse
> To take their rest in heliconian glades,
> To glory in the laurel's pensive shades?
> Such immortality's expensive price
> Is labor, wrought with ceaseless sacrifice.
> Ambition for a bard's undying fame
> Becomes, alas, of simple peace the bane.

We seek—I too!—a palm whose fruit is sorrow,
As if from deathless verse we life could borrow,
As if undying words could breath bestow
To sarcous remnants clothed in dust below.
Note well that fame, though long endure it may,
And last beyond this vagrant life's brief day,
Is but true immortality's false shade,
And from mere insubstantial words is made.

To sing in golden voice, to sound the lyre
With all that high Parnassus may inspire,
Are works, indeed, of sweet felicity,
But lead to naught of true eternity.
Not erudition's depth but virtue's grace
Secures the soul in blissful peace a place;
Yea, piety, not learning, God shall weigh
Upon that dreaded final Judgement Day.

But they who learning and good deeds unite,
With twofold wings, shall blithely take their flight;
Their names the Muses will inscribe in stone;
Their souls in Light divine shall find a home!

The Agitation of the Depraved Soul, Compared with the Quiet Peace of the Righteous

When fearsome Ares—bloody god of war!—
Upon the land his crimson wine doth pour,
And strikes us with his gore-encrusted fist,
By ulvine madness feeble souls are kissed
And grow to lust for death, to long for slaughter;
To gaze on precious blood as if mere water!
In such ensanguined times, dark Eris reigns;
Usurious monopoly Mars claims,
As sacred temples burn unto the ground,
And congeries of broken limbs abound,
And salty blood makes wastelands of the earth,
While plenty's superseded by gaunt dearth.

And chill it is when blows yon arctic gale
Which tempest brings, with nubivagant hail,
Which, scornful of the grower's anxious care,
Does strip the vine of purple riches bare.
And just so is the soul infused with pride,
Which discontented ever must abide,
And seeks by rabid conflict and by war
Its own advancement—vainly!—to ensure.

Mount Etna, armed with foul hephaestic breath,
Does vomit forth her noxious fumes of death,
And spittle, rank with harsh acridity,
Pour outs upon the valley and the lea;
Malign, it—void of reason and distinction—
Seeks naught but light and life's complete extinction.
Thus does the fire of wrath burn in our hearts,
And seldom is extinguished once it starts;
For little can avert its ardent power,
Save holy virtue's cool, becalming shower
Or time's unfailing panaceic balm,
Which, either soon or late, restores blest calm.

The ocean waves, lo, beckon temptingly
To set one's craft afloat, and recklessly
To distant shores to strive, for gold or fame—
There, siren-promised treasuries to gain.
But, merciless, the turgid waters thunder
And waves of tumult swell in awesome wonder,
To rend and tear the hapless bark asunder
And draw its panicked crew, resisting, under
The water's crushing weight, to ocean bed
Where, on them, carp and crab are duly fed.
And thus does vain Ambition, haughty, call
The avaricious heart—it to enthrall,
That, seeking glory, it does peril court;
And but for peril, shall attain thus naught.

But for the pious heart, which is replete
With presence of the holy Paraclete,
Tranquility secure shall always be
Its lot; though all around it may the sea
With tumid vortex viciously abound,
Whilst skies with eldritch thunder do resound.
The innocent of heart shall truly know
The clement sunshine's cupreous, warm glow;
And Heaven's undisturbed felicity
Shall their companion faithful ever be.

On the Birthday of Christ our Lord

O most beloved Infant! Thou wert born
Whilst hoary winter reigned with air forlorn,
And in the rude abode which saw thy birth
Burnt neither homely fire nor warming hearth.
But rather thou assumed a state most poor,
Thy tender body resting on harsh straw,
And under humble roof didst thou lie shiv'ring
While round thee played the frigid breezes, quiv'ring.
That sable night was void of stellar glow,
And thus thou entered to this zone below.
Indeed, no place within this fictile sphere
Could ever dare approach, nor venture near,
That worthy of the honor it should be
Thy head thereon to rest befittingly.

O Lord, thou thereby teach that we mere mortals,
Desirous of ingress to Heaven's portals,
Must choose not things exalted, but the lowly;
For true humility is truly holy.

But—lo!—now Phoebus, brilliant, is reborn,
Arises the new year with lustrous dawn.
As wakened Janus ancient bolts unlocks,
The Year, renewed, beseeching entrance, knocks.

In thy nativity, pleromic Lord,
Earth's pristine vim and vigor are restored!
Enlightened by the wonder of thy birth
Humanity rejoices, filled with mirth;
And never shall we cease to glorify
And worship thee, true Sun who shine on high!

Hymn to the Divine Spirit

O Spirit, beauty of celestial grace!
Thou holy breath of vast, sidereal space;
Thrice sacrosanct, thou Ghost of living flame;
Thrice hallowed, whisper of th'eternal Name.
O Paraclete resplendent, hither come,
Who can tartarean hordes so overcome,
That pavid fiends of hell shall quail with fear—
To my faint heart as guardian-flame draw near!

Uncreated force, and potency
Coeval with sublime Divinity,
The love connecting Father and the Son,
The sacrament who make the Godhead one,
The radiant flare of deathless charity,
The luminance of Wisdom's mystery,
The sweetest refuge of all care-worn minds,
The ardor which the soul to Heaven binds!
O come! Into my heart depth's gently pour
Thy lucent love, by which I may adore
Unseen eternity's infinitude—
Of bliss, the all-surpassing plenitude!

O, Thou it was whose overshad'wing presence
United, in the Virgin's womb, the essence
Divine with human nature; so thus giving
New hope, redemptive balm unto the living.
Unite, we pray, us to eternity,
Let us enjoy deific liberty!

The mind which is bereft of thy sublime,
Illuminating presence, must repine
Amidst the gloomy tempest of this life,
As prey to ceaseless doubt and endless strife,
And, as a tree uncultivated, grow,
That nary may it bud nor blossom show;
But as a garden, withered by the black
And phlegethonic heat, perforce must lack
Both amber fruit and warmly purpling flower,
Deprived of Gaia's vivifying power.

Endowed with blessings of supernal grace,
Though, is that one in whom thou take thy place,
In whom the amaranthine bloom of love
Is sown by Spirit-breath from realms above.
As fragrant frangipanis freshly flourish
When Heaven's imbrous dewfall them doth nourish,
Ev'n thus dost thou the human mind refine,
That never fleshly bonds shall it confine
To mundane things; or carnal lethargy
Shall rule it, but, instead, supremely free,
It wanders through nephelean plains of space,
In heights empyreal to assume its place.

Thrice sacrosanct, thou Ghost of living flame;
Thrice hallowed, whisper of th'eternal Name.
O Paraclete resplendent, come to me
And lead me hence to thine eternity!

The Sun and the Bee

O Bee, arrayed in xanthic, fiery robe,
Thou seem to imitate the solar globe,
Which reigns unrivalled in the turquoise sky,
Traversing, bright, the firmament on high.
And like great Sol, thou pour forth gold in measure;
He, day's expanse of light; thou, honeyed pleasure.
Of thee, too, luminosity is born,
When wax, the candle's substance, thou dost form.
Why envy thou proud Phoebus, little Bee?
For God who made the Sun made also thee.

On the Engagement Ring of the Blessed Virgin Mary, Reverently Preserved in the City of Perugia

The rainbow's banner proffers us a sign,
A deixis of fealty divine,
By which a holy promise earth did gain
That nevermore, with dark, torrential rain,
Would God act to destroy poor Adam's race,
And leave bereft of life the planet's face.

But greater far the glories of thee spoken—
O privileged Ring!—whereby was once betoken
The blest betrothal of the Deity
To Heaven's Queen, the Empress maidenly,
The Virgin-Mother, *Logos*-fecund spouse,
The temple of the Lord, the Savior's house
Of purest gold and mystic ivory,
The flow'r of hope, the true star of the sea.

Yea, stygian waters never shall we fear,
Whilst thou, our purer Venus, linger near!

On the Work of Cardinal Robert Bellarmine, *The Ascension of the Mind into God*

Deceptively do vanities assume
The guise of highest goods and greatest boons,
To lure poor, guileless minds into their snares,
And then to plague them with distress and cares;
And, worse, distract them from the goods above,
For realms of peace and glory, and from love
Of God, the One eternal destiny
Of souls from carnal bondage rendered free.
And when, with feignéd sweetness, flesh doth fail
To tempt the heart, then tries it to assail
The mind with anxious troubles and with fear,
That scarce to it th'olympian light appears.
By either mundane lusts or worries caught,
The soul for things eternal spares no thought.

And many mortal worldlings here are known
To seek false immortality in stone,
Vast edifices raising to the skies,
As if—poor fools!—by doing thus thereby
They paradisic ingress may attain,
The glorious bliss which bides therein to gain.
And there are minds, misguided, who apprise,
By verse, not stone, to gain a deathless prize,
Enrolled amongst the poets, laurel-crowned,
Who for their well-wrought lyrics win renown,
And for their words of mnemosynic fire
The laud of choirs parnassian do inspire.
Yet such fame, elevated though it be,
Is but mimesis of eternity.

For, struck with death, whom no one may evade,
The great, applauded, learnéd, all are made
The equals of the simple and the poor—
Subjected, all, to Clotho's changeless law.
Their mortal substance is reduced to bones—
Its praise and fame unlike to it unknown.
And if, perchance, its fame or human glory
Be told posthumously, an empty story
It is unto the soul from hence now gone,
Who no more to this orb terrene belongs.

Alas, what dense miasmas yet oppress
The human throng with bleak unhappiness!
Desire and fear, attachment, pride and lust
Weigh down the spirit, cleaving to the dust!
As all the multitude of flowing streams
To ocean go, but never does it seem
That Neptune's briny drink shall overflow,
So not from passing goods thy soul may know
Full satisfaction, or its true contentment;
But sorrow, anger, avarice, resentment,
Shall plague it while it loves this ebbing dust,
And to such fleeting shades its hope entrusts.

Despise, O Friend, all things that pass away!
From earth's temptations, turn thy gaze this day.
It was with eyes tight shut to mundane scenes
The Jacob once beheld, in cryptic dream,
A ladder reaching to the realms on high,
Extending past the firmament of sky,
Yea, past the welkin's amethystine dome
Unto ethereal meads of light unknown.
And 'twas in equipage of fiery state
That blest Elijah flew though Heaven's gate.

So Bellarmine's fine tome—if thou but read—
Thy soul to mystic Truth will surely lead,
And contemplation's golden path will teach,
And place eidetic bliss within thy reach!

Ode for St. Mary Magdalene

Enticing Pleasure! O seductress sweet!
With glist'ning wings, adornéd thy lithe feet,
By which thou fly the globe with merry haste
And proffer to the tongue the merest of taste
Of nenuphar's intoxicating wine.
Each heart, enthralled, then longs: "O were she mine!"
More lethal than the basilisk thy kiss,
But paltry price—reck they—for such rare bliss.
But never art thou held secure or fast,
For thy sweet blandishments but fleetly last.

What venoms thou dost keep, concealed within!
Mellifluous the nectar of thy sin.
Thy purring whispers speak unto the flesh,
And souls unwary deftly do enmesh.
More lovely than the rose, thy tempting bloom;
More certain than the tigress, thy dark doom!
O lily ophic, sweet narcotic scent;
Ambrosial thy taste, yet from hell sent!
To thee, both kings and prophets did succumb;
Lord Solomon the Wise was overcome,
And prudent David, too, could not resist—
By asphodelian beauty, darkly kissed.

O Magdalen, of pulchritude supreme,
Surpassing every yearning, heart-wrought dream!
Both instrument and victim wert thou to
Soft pleasure's sweet, inebriating dew.
Lo, what most artful and accomplished care
Didst thou bestow on form and dress and hair,
That beauty's perfect image thou might be,
That lustful eyes should be inflamed by thee!
Thou loved but to be loved by all indeed;
That every man should want thee was thy need.

But then a higher Beauty did design
Thy love of love with mercy to refine,
That thence thy heart would should burn incessantly
With love for that sublime Divinity,
Who is the source of beauty and of love,
The Word of Life, incarnate from above,
The Son of God, and Deity supreme,
Compared to whom, all else is but a dream.
Through heinous sin's dense clouds of plumbeous dark,
Appeared *he* as the iridescent arc,
The rainbow, banner of Pandora's treasure
Of hope benign, of mercy's fulgid measure.

Behold! This beauteous penitent did fall
In love with Love made flesh, to be blest thrall
Of Heaven's glorious Son, and His beloved,
The flames of sins by passions' tears now smothered.
O erstwhile courtesan, graced to repent,
To thee has newfound love and virtue lent
The topaz luminance of radiant day,
Which drives the haze of guilty lust away.
Thy crœsean lucre earned by prostitution
Is purged now by a lachrymose solution;
Thy pearls, made nacreous drops of plangent pain,
Which flow forth even as a silvern rain.
His feet, which trod the bright elysian fields,
Now to thy tender laving gently yield.
And with thy hair, of lustre like to silk,
And with thy hand, of whiteness like to milk,
Thou cleansed away the sin of wasted years,
Illumined now by sapience of tears.

And, Magdalene, how faithfully thou followed,
In union with thy Love, thy liege, to swallow
The tetric gall of hardship and despair,
Its shadow cast upon thy visage fair!
For at the cross thou stood and sorely wept,
As vigil there in agony thou kept,
And at the tomb's mute stones of leaden gray
Thou waited, in unhope, for dismal day;
Yet witnessed first the truly risen Lord,
The flavid Dawn, most by thy heart adored;
The orient Star—chatoyant, sacral, bright!—
Revealed unto thy love-enraptured sight.

Thrice blessèd thou, dryadic thegn of Light
Divine—disperser of sin's umbrous night,
Of mortal darkness and of fleshly gloom;
Effulgence of the sun and of the moon;
The beauty which is immortality:
Thy deathless love, his true Divinity!

On a Statue of the Huntress Goddess Diana by a Fountain

Through emerald walds, Thou, O sweet Deity,
Hast trod with damask-shod alacrity;
In venatorial chase, to fugent deer,
By canine horde companioned, hast'ning near;
Accepting now, by febrile flight fatigued,
Beside this fountain, slumber's well-earned meed:
In honeyed somnolence—serene and deep—
Thou tastest nect'rous benison of sleep.

O Goddess virginal, huntress celestial,
Thou sylvan empress, chastest maiden vestal!
I credit not that thy form I behold
Be lifeless, fashioned but of marble cold!
For feel I not thy dulcet breath's pulsations?
Perceive I not thy limbs' meek tremulations?
Or is it just the water's vitreous spray
Which on my longing's fancy thus does play?

Selected Poetry of Pope Alexander VII

Anaxiphórminges húmnoi,
tína theón, tín' héroa, tína d' ándra keladésomen?
—Pindar, *Olympic Ode II*

O Hymns sublime, who reign with vatic lyre,
Igniting phorminx with pieridean fire!—
What god, what hero, or what deeds of fame,
Shall we with lays sanctiloquent proclaim?

What mysteries does Fabio Chigi's noble poetry convey?
Whence comes this fresh, radiant light of novel inspiration?
It is, indeed, as if some Heavenly siren had fashioned a new divine
canticle, whereby the secrets of the gods are now conveyed to this lower
sphere of earth . . .
—Apollonius Florens (*floruit XVII saeculo*)

To Poetry

    I'll follow not the stirring call of arms,
    Nor clarion blasts resounding fierce alarms,
    Nor promises of treasuries untold
    Awaiting for the navigator bold.
    But rather lulling tones of rippling rills
    My heart with gentler motions now do fill.
    Nor martial praise, nor bloodied victories,
    This poet's soul could evermore appease.
    No gold of Midas, gleaming and yet cold,
    Could ever my affections truly hold.

    For those ambitious for this world's vain things
    But hasten on of victrix Death her sting.
    Those who the gaudy show of glory choose
    Life's peaceful days and calmest moments lose.
    The harp's irenic plectrum will serve best
    As company to me in hours of rest,
    Whilst dancing languid over melic string
    To make the air with placid musings ring.

    Let not the gloomy cypress nor dark tomb
    Remind me of all flesh's destined doom.
    Instead may hills, refreshed by Zephyr's kiss,
    Be my theatre of untroubled bliss.
    For what is life indeed but one great song,
    A stream which wanders ceaselessly along?
    A glass of Lethe's wine, an ode of Horace,
    Serve me as anodyne, suffice for solace.

On the Day of the Annunciation of the Conception of the Lord to the Blessed Virgin Mary

The clouds, whose opaque gloom obscures this sphere
Of earth, with trembling haste now disappear.
The tempest, whose dark majesty once towered
In welkin heights, takes flight, made trepid coward.
And peace, kind gift of Heaven's gracious Lord,
Unto the orb telluric is restored.
Aeolic breezes rouse the lambent air,
And, roseate, Apollo's dew-drenched glare
Upon the sward's tsavorite arras glows,
As Pan serotinal largesse bestows.

Then rich, carnelian tones the sky displays
As gleam the gloaming's soft vesperic rays.
Enthroned, divine Love from Parnassus reigns;
To kiss fair Maiden Earth, descending, deigns;
Just as a bridegroom, set, by love, alight,
Now hitherward from astral leas takes flight,
And into Mary's womb, in flesh encased,
Amongst humanity takes humble place—
A zeph'rous spark, renewing all creation,
With mystic dawn of glorious liberation!

On the Election of Urban VIII as Pope

Just as the radiant, light-engirded King
Of Heaven, does dispose each cosmic thing
According to his sapience supernal,
And separates the night from hours diurnal,
That Erebus and Phoebus each display
Their robes of dark and light in due array;
And gelid winter, with its glacial cold,
At his behest, its fury does withhold,
That myrtle-crowned and orange-tinted spring
Its arborescent arabesques may bring,
And waxing summer's coruscating glow,
Its fulvid face, frugiferous, may show.
Thus all things in this cosmic symphony
Entwine, with dithyrambic harmony.

And so, by providential disposition,
A pontiff apt and glorious now is risen!
Pope Urban shines as Helios at new dawn,
The day-star from the orient ocean born;
Yea, flooding earth with vivifying blaze,
Whilst warming tepid hearts with fervent rays!
With sanctity and faith and modesty,
This thrice-crowned potentate resplends, and he
With innocence of purest, Opeth gold,
Restores of aureate peace the tranquil hold.
His soul—note thou—is fixed on Truth divine,
Elixir rare which does the mind refine:
The gonfalon of God thus shall him guide,
Untouched by ought of avarice or pride.

The anchor serves the storm-tossed craft to save,
To hold secure amidst tritonic waves;
So thus will serve our Heaven-destined pope,
A beacon of serene, celestial hope!
Hark thou! The skies with strains rhapsodic ring;
The cherub host themselves his paeons sing!

Inscription for an Unnamed Tomb I

O thou who pass this tomb, pause now to hear;
Unto these silent stones lend silent ear;
Though I—whose mortal bones within abide—
From hence have long since, in my essence, hied.
Seek not to know my rank, nor fate, nor name;
Enquire not thou of monument nor fame.
But let it be sufficient unto thee,
This tomb—my lasting palace—here to see.
Seize thou the day! For with each moment past,
Grim death, upon thy heels, approaches fast.

Inscription for an Unnamed Tomb II

    Whatever, in the form of anxious care,
    Upon this world's ephem'ral stage thou bear;
    Whatever lusts, emprises, hopes and schemes,
    Thou nourish in thy heart, or in thy dreams—
    In such a tomb as this will be their end,
    When death thy soul shall to its judgement send.
    But now thy earthly battle must continue;
    So gird thyself! With muscle and with sinew
    Of steely strength; be ready for thy foe,
    That in the end thou victory may know.
    The horrent hydra of temptation grim,
    The soporific lotus of sweet sin,
    With prayer thou'll conquer; and shalt overcome
    The tomb's drear dungeon, and, just as the sun
    Resurgent, in thy triumph thence arise,
    Ascending to receive thy Heav'nly prize!

On a Copy of Caesar's *Commentaries* which has been Gnawed by a Mouse

Why should the budding author lend his care
His texts with studied polish to prepare,
When, in the ebon hours while Nyx holds sway,
Some brazen rodent gnaws the page away?
A mouse concealed, with bold temerity,
Destroys lines worthy of eternity;
With fretful maw, erases thoughts august,
Reducing deathless musings unto dust!

O Time, voracious carnifex of all,
Beholding, in due course, each empire's fall!
Lo, more pernicious is this mouse than thee—
Consuming poor ol' Caesar greedily!

On Water Turning into Stone, and Stone into Water

Behold how water, in its flow persistent,
Erodes the stone, initially resistant;
By patience overcoming marble's vigor,
And soft'ning, by degrees, its stubborn rigor.
And see how then the stream, when it does settle
Into some swamp or pond of miry mettle,
Shall harden first to mud and then to clay,
To petrify to stone, one parching day.

What will not Time's vast sweep in due course alter?—
Transmuting adamantine stone to water,
And through stagnation, water back to stone,
By processes of Nature quite unknown!

So marvel not if tears which, warmly felt,
Cause flinty hearts in piety to melt;
Nor wonder, too, if fury or black hate
A feeble heart to granite does mutate!

On Rome

O Rome! Thou glory of the zone terrene
And fane refulgent with the Light supreme,
Before whom potentates ought genuflect,
Whose argent turrets astral gleams reflect!

Impassive Fate herself does fear thy name,
For neither barb'rous sword nor rampant flame
Possess capacity whereby to harm thee,
Nor threat, nor deed sufficient to alarm thee!
We've witnessed, as the aeons run their courses,
Thee plagued by Barathron's nefandous forces.
We've witnessed, raised in hate, tartarean fire;
Apostate chieftains, galled with orcic ire,
Against thee, rabid curs of war unchain,
Ascendancy—O vain hope!—thus to gain.

Yet out of all such trials and fell disasters
Thou risest new, in weal and beauty vaster—
Yea—like the Phoenix, from the ashes born,
Or like Apollo, surging with the dawn!

Rejoice, O ark of grace, eternal Rome,
Who serve God's cosmic church as sacral throne!

Meditation on the Nativity of Christ

Lo, when the Son divine descended to
This sphere sublunar, all things to renew,
Sent forth from vaults sidereal to embrace
The flesh-enbound condition of our race,
A lonely shepherd, sage and hoar and old,
Who on the braes of Bethel grazed his fold,
His eyes the welkin's portents did survey
And numinously loquent, thus did say:
"O sacred Son of Heaven, hope of earth!
Thou long-awaited Christ-child, now thy birth
Approaches, to unbind sin's heavy chains,
Refreshing weary earth with crystal rain!
Word increate made flesh, whose majesty
The light purpureal clothes in brilliancy,
To whom the swains seraphic bend their knee,
Perceiving in thy form Divinity!
O blest the fault whereby to us did come
A Savior—God himself and God's true Son!"

Thus spake he, and anon to him was giv'n
Response in utt'rance from the cyan Heav'n,
In clarion voice was heard yon wingéd throng,
United in effulgence of high song:
"O, glory be to God, the star-throned King!
Let all creation, trembling, homage bring!
Let peace supernal echo endlessly
The silent name of God's eternity!
He comes, the Deity's supreme perfection—
He comes, the earthen realm's hope of redemption!"

With such exalted heralds, holy Child,
Why dost thou show thyself as infant mild?
Why lie supine in beddings of the poor,
Wrapped not in samite silk, but laid on straw?
The cruel decembral winds now, ruthless, blow;
Descends on thee the algid fall of snow.

Beside mute ox and ass, a maiden waits,
Attentive but to thee; she contemplates
Deep eleusinian secrets of God's love,
Imparted by the Spirit's flame-plumed dove.

Now rest thyself, O Child, in the embrace
Of thy blithe Mother, Mary, Queen of grace.
Enjoy consoling warmth, whilst yet thou may,
For gray Gethsemane's not far away,
Nor yet the knoll of blood-black Calvary,
Where thou shalt mount that fateful gallows tree!

Dear Child, permit me, please, to be so bold
Thy infant form, in sinful arms, to hold,
Caressing thee, perhaps, with greater love
Than felt I yet for all the Heav'ns above!

Meditation on the Passion of the Savior I: '*Ecce Homo*'

Behold the Man! And see the Deity,
Who reigns in unbound light's infinity,
Now spurned and struck by cold, perfidious hands;
Circumfluent, the crowd derisive stands.
A shower of blood his pallid face bedews,
And scourges slash his alabaster thews.
The scornful scepter takes he in his hand—
Which healed the leper, made the lame to stand.
And from his eyes—whose glance the stars obey—
Flow glaucous tears, of tincture leaden gray.
A cloak, with blood of oyster purple-hued,
Is placed on arms whose pow'r the spheres subdued.
Behold, the thorns—at his behest created—
Entwined to form a crown, whose spines, unsated,
Imbibe with xeric thirst that blood divine,
In which is hid Omnipotence sublime.

This scepter, giv'n as token of disdain,
Bespeaks but of our sin-begotten pain.
The purple robe—a garment bearing scorn—
Reveals our weight of wretchedness forlorn.
The crown—which seeks to mock the living Lord—
But marks the One by seraph hosts adored!

Meditation on the Passion of the Savior II:
In the Garden of Gethsemane

Alas! What multitude of tears must flow
The merest fragment of my woes to show?
Or what heart-broken, elegiac dirge
Could serve my melancholic mood to purge?

And yet Christ willed, by clemency enthralled,
To cleanse, by pain, the atrous stains of all
This race of Adam's wretched progeny,
Restoring, underserved, our liberty.
Just as it was within a garden's glade
That first was tasted that which Law forbade,
Yea, so it was a garden which first saw
The Savior's blood, in agony, to pour,
As haemic globes of caustic, acrid sweat,
In carmine streamlets, leaving soil wet
With blood divine, and sweat, and saline tears—
Effusion of the gall of holy fears.
Shall God—for he *is* God—thus sadly sigh?
Shall high Divinity consent to cry?
Yet here he is—behold—in solitude,
Before whom quakes th'angelic multitude!

Yet soon the crowds malign shall gather round
To look upon him, scourged, and by thorns crowned;
To see his blood, as sacral purple, flow;
To see his wounds, as royal rubies, glow.
But now the trait'rous horde approaches nigh
With clubs and swords and torches, and with lies.
O, better they had never seen the light;
Yea, better sunk in blind, meontic night!

But from this song I, silent, must refrain;
Too weak am I to contemplate his pain.

A Prayer to God Imploring his Assistance

> Within the secret chamber of mine heart,
> I hear the gospel word its Truth impart:
> "The one who shall my footsteps humbly tread
> Will not be conquered by the darkness dread."
> O Lord, walk thou as kindly friend to me,
> And to my steps a trusted light e'er be.
> Without thee, lo, I stumble and I fall;
> Thy strength, thy love, thy wisdom be mine all!

An Inscription for a Tomb Composed in the Style of the Tenth Century

O, Hearken to my words, and in them trust!
Why dost thou pride thyself, thou bairn of dust?
Behold, the dismal remnants thou here see,
Thou too, one coming day, wilt, certes, be!
All time-bound glory Momus shall erase;
Repute and riches, pow'r, prestige and praise
Shall be extinguished, to oblivion cast;
But two things only past the grave shall last—
First, sins and deeds of swart thou hast committed
Or pious duties ruefully omitted,
And, second, works of holy charity;
These two—thy good and bad—shall go with thee!

And God, upon his dreaded judgement throne,
The sentence will pronounce in thund'rous tone:
"Away from me, accursèd!" unto some;
To others, "Blessèd, to my kingdom come!"
And such alone will claim reality;
Each eidolon of mortal vanity
Shall as the spell of Morpheus then seem—
Yea, naught more than phantasmagoric dream.

So choose now, which thou wilt; foul hell or Heav'n?
According to thy deeds will it be giv'n!

A Note Accompanying a Cat,
Given as a Gift to a Young Woman

(Written prior to his ordination to the sacred ministry)

To thee, O Mistress sweet, I bear a gift
Which happily thy soul, I'll trow, will lift—
A tender feline, playful in its joy,
Surpassing, as diversion, any toy!
Yet think it not, Dear, just a pretty face—
Amongst the wise and brave it earns its place,
For silently it goes from here to there,
With tacit tread, absorbing all with care,
And making perspicacious observation,
Assessing with astute discrimination.

And graceful though it be and prone to play,
It tarries not the hyrax gray to slay.
With whimsical caprice it's wont to kill,
To toss the mouse or bird around at will!
And gen'rously it likes to share each treat;
To offer, at its mistress's sweet feet,
Each little living morsel it has caught,
As if in some great school of manners taught.
And though its lineage may be obscure,
Its graceful gait its breeding does ensure.
With just, perhaps, the slighted touch of pride,
Its noble rank it scarcely strives to hide.

It's beauty, too, is such to rival thine,
With eyes which like pearlescent stars do shine,
And pretty ears of shell-like, elfin slightness,
And pirouetting steps of fairy lightness.
As ebony, its coat is black as night,
With feet and mouth adorned with candent white.
And when it deems it time to take a nap,
'Twill seek, my Dear, the refuge of thy lap.

And if this little gift shall calm thy sorrow,
I'll bring another one to thee tomorrow!
Yes, if thou should this cat come to adore,
I'll bring thee one, or two—or twenty more!

A Note Accompanying a Rose
Given as a Gift to a Young Woman

(Written prior to his ordination to the sacred ministry)

    Accept, O Maid, this rose of scarlet red,
    Which has upon my tears and sighs been fed;
    My tears and sighs which for thee long did flow
    This noble blossom—yea—have caused to grow.
    O! may it bring unto thy cheek a bloom,
    A glimpse of which, the Cosmos would illume!
    And to thine eyes—a sparkling, opal gleam,
    Before which moon and stars would dismal seem.
    And may it grant, 'twixt thee and me, a kiss,
    To rival very Heaven's perfect bliss!
    And may it coo as gentle as the dove
    Confessing in thy tender ear my love.

A Pilgrimage to a Shrine of the Virgin Mary

O Queen of noblest blood and royal line,
Most worthy of imperium sublime;
Of Triune Deity the spouse and Mother,
And gracious daughter, loved beyond all other;
Best refuge of the sorrowful and poor,
Whom vestal choirs, with tend'rest love, adore!
To thee, sweet Maid, my heart enraptured flies,
And sees in thee the azure of the skies,
The wealth of earth, and ocean's sapphire treasure,
With joy transcending every bound and measure.

Thy temple shall I seek in nephrite hills,
Where sylvan beauty ardent senses thrills.
For naught else so infatuates my heart!
No earthly maid such passion can impart.
Esteem I more to serve as thrall to thee,
Than suzerainty of earth and sky and sea.
For whoso knows the grace of thy regard,
Against sin's bane possesses surest guard.

Through thee, mine All, Love's quiddity did shine—
That Love which is thy Jesus, King divine;
Whose flesh affixéd was unto the rood,
Whose blood, as vermeil dewfall, earth renewed.
That infant God did in thine arms recline,
Did fix his eyes' infinitude on thine,
And found his choicest place of holy rest,
Upon the iv'ry bed of thy sweet breast.

And so, as pilgrim, hie I to thy fane,
In hope, sweet mercy's benison to gain.
And there, upon thy threshold, shall I weep,
Precations plangent pour forth at thy feet;
And kiss the ground thy presence sanctifies,
And pray—O!—not with words, but with my sighs.

www.ingramcontent.com/pod-product-compliance
Lightning Source LLC
Chambersburg PA
CBHW061511040426
42450CB00008B/1569